Colorful Creatures Exotic Ocean Fish

By Jordan Biggio

As a bonus each exotic ocean fish is printed twice in this book. Not only does this give you the opportunity to color each scene twice, it also gives you a clean slate in case you make a mistake! It is like having two copies of the same book.

As a second bonus, the type of each fish is printed on the back of the page. Not only does this provide you with the name of each exotic fish but you can use this information to easily see what each fish really looks like. Some of these fish have some really wild color patterns!

Thank you for purchasing a copy of my book. I had a great time creating this book for you and I would to see what you do with the designs. Feel free to email me images of what you have colored. My email address is:

jordanbiggio@gmail.com

If you enjoyed coloring my designs, then please leave a review to let others know what you thought, be it good or bad. Leaving a review is the single best way to help support me and my art. Leaving a review is easy and don't forget to post a completed colored page with your review.

Thanks again!

ISBN-13: 978-1534909571
ISBN-10: 1534909575

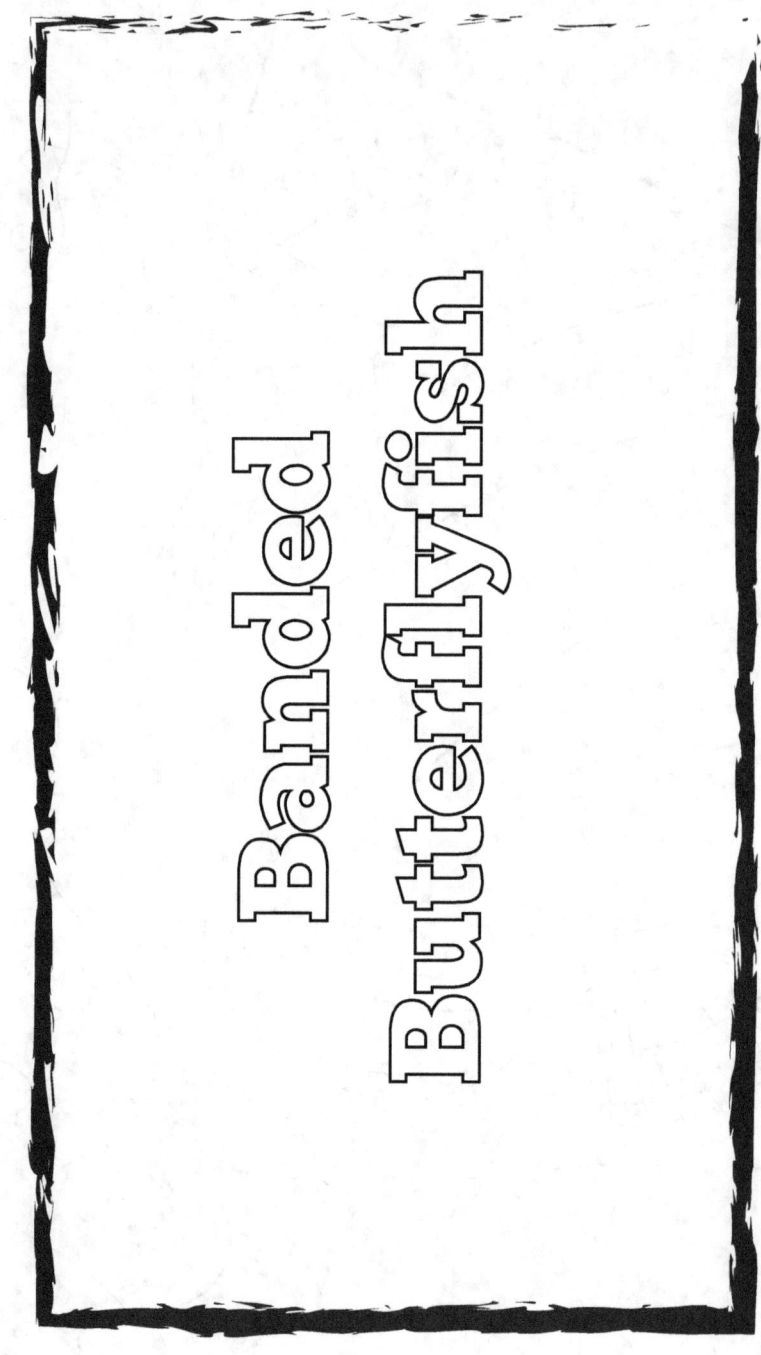

Banded Butterflyfish

Bluehead Wrasse

Blue Tang

Cardinalfish

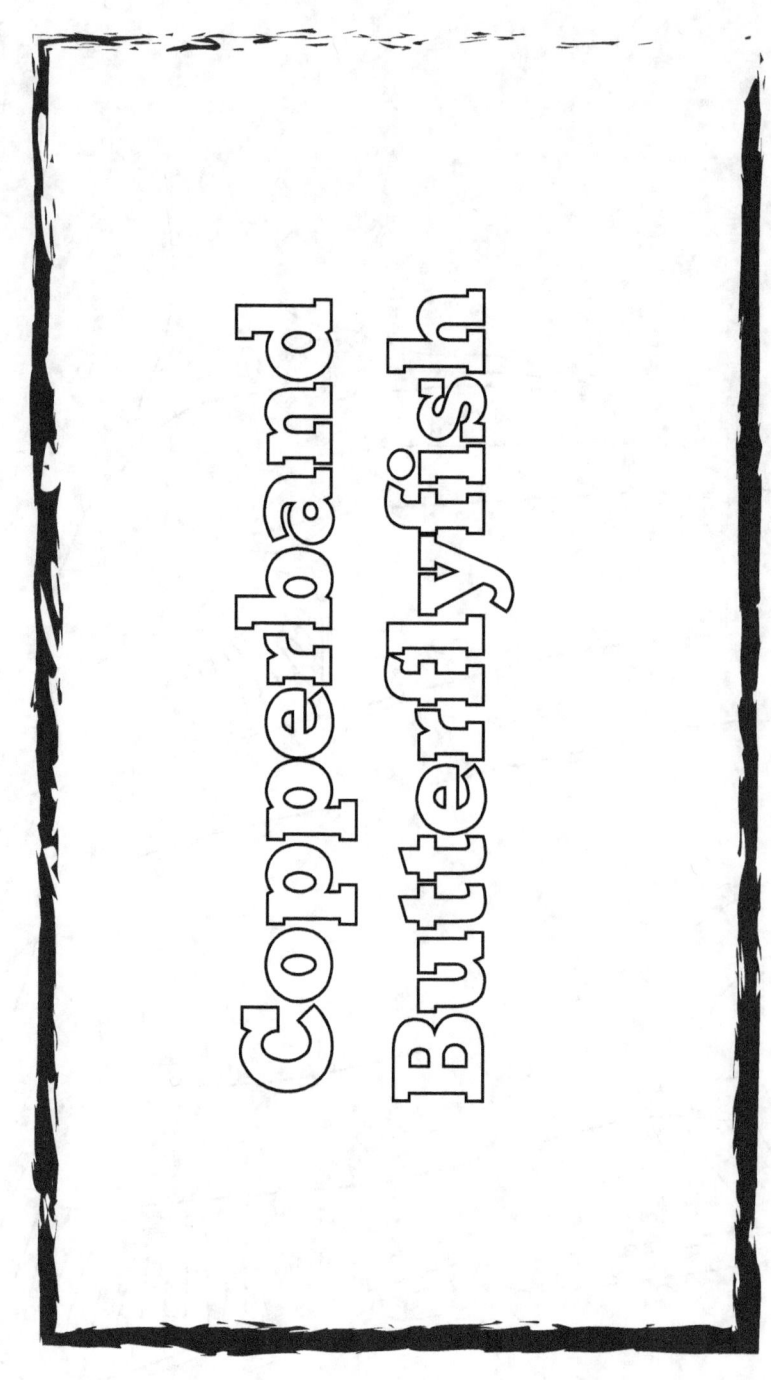

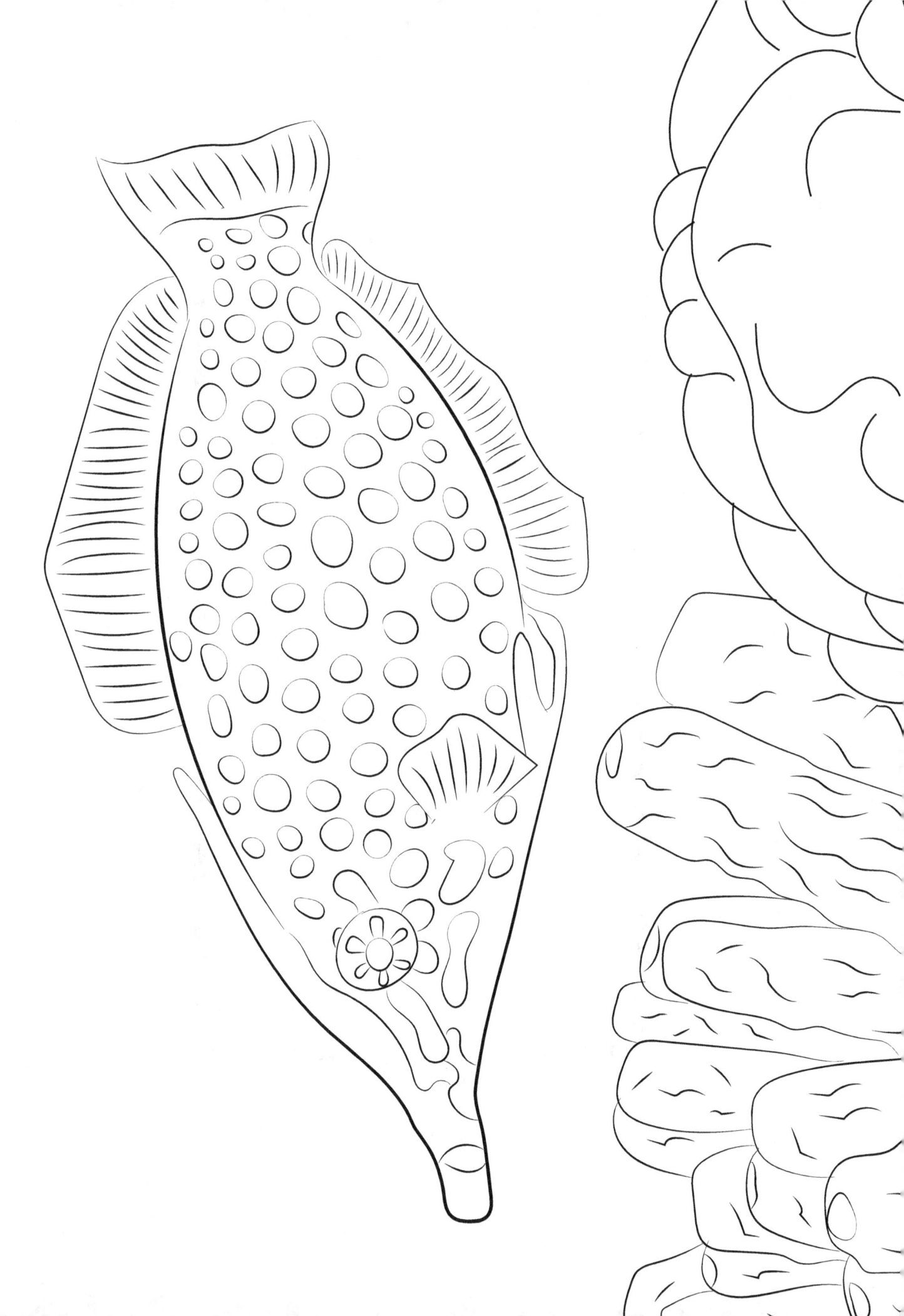

Flame Angelfish

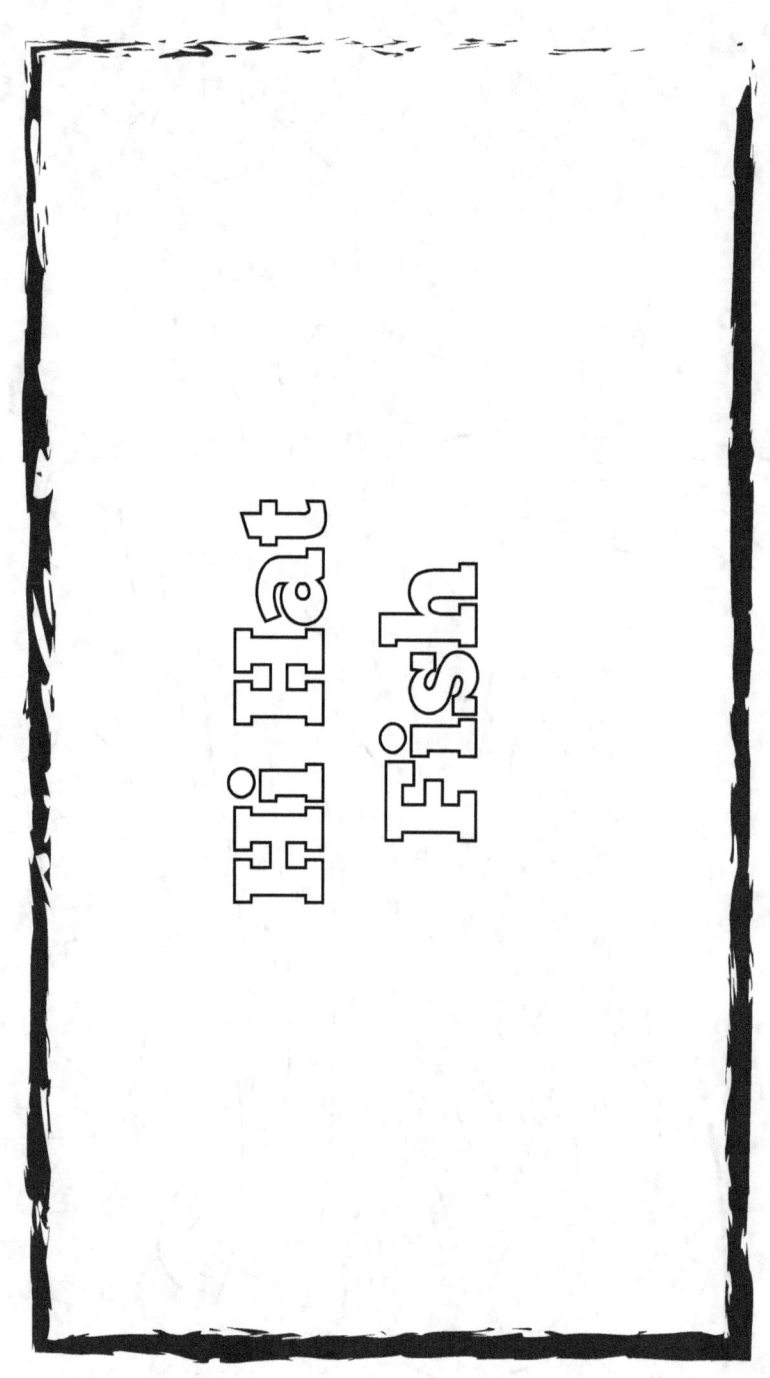

Lionfish

Moorish Idol
Fish

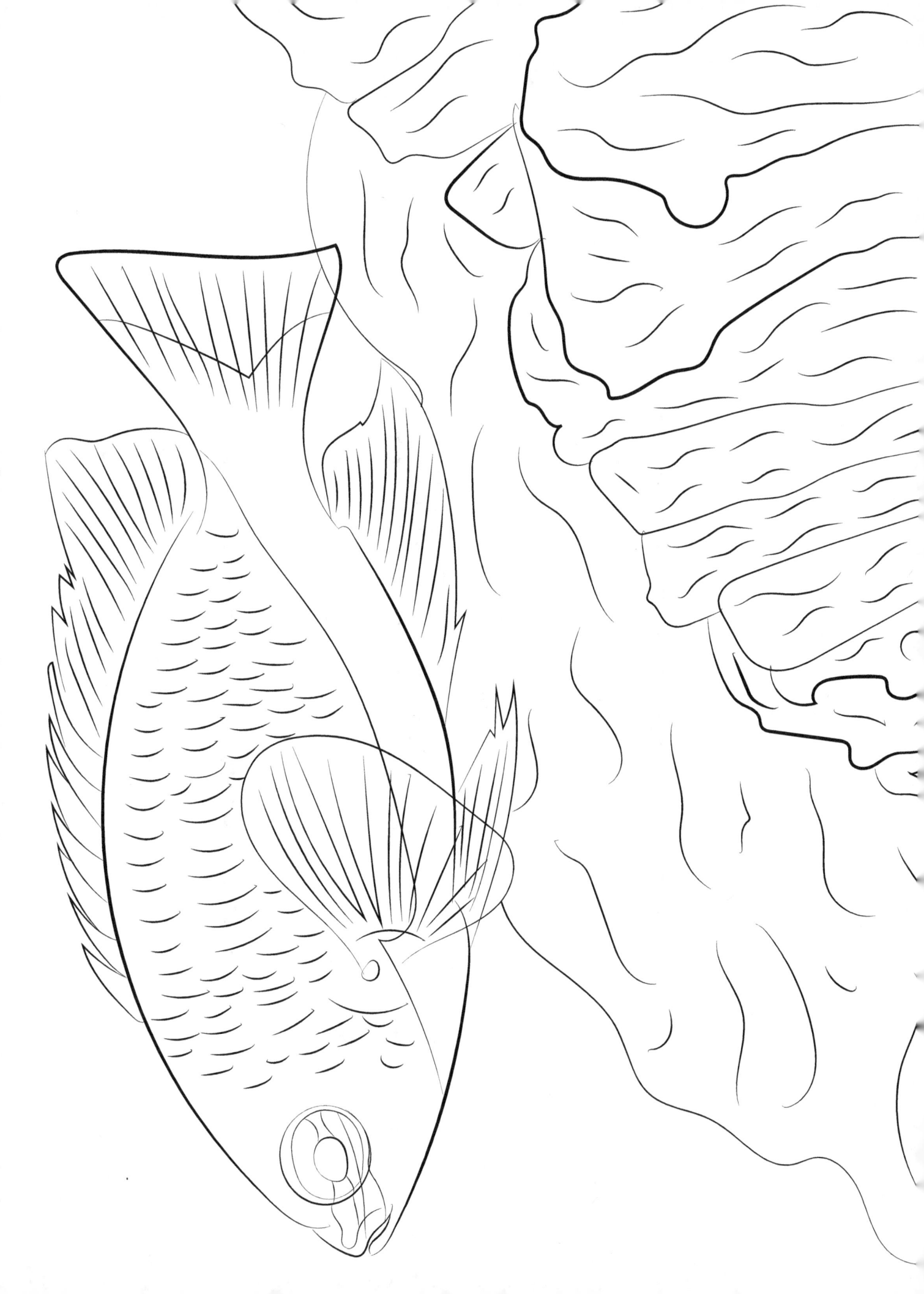

Pennant Coralfish

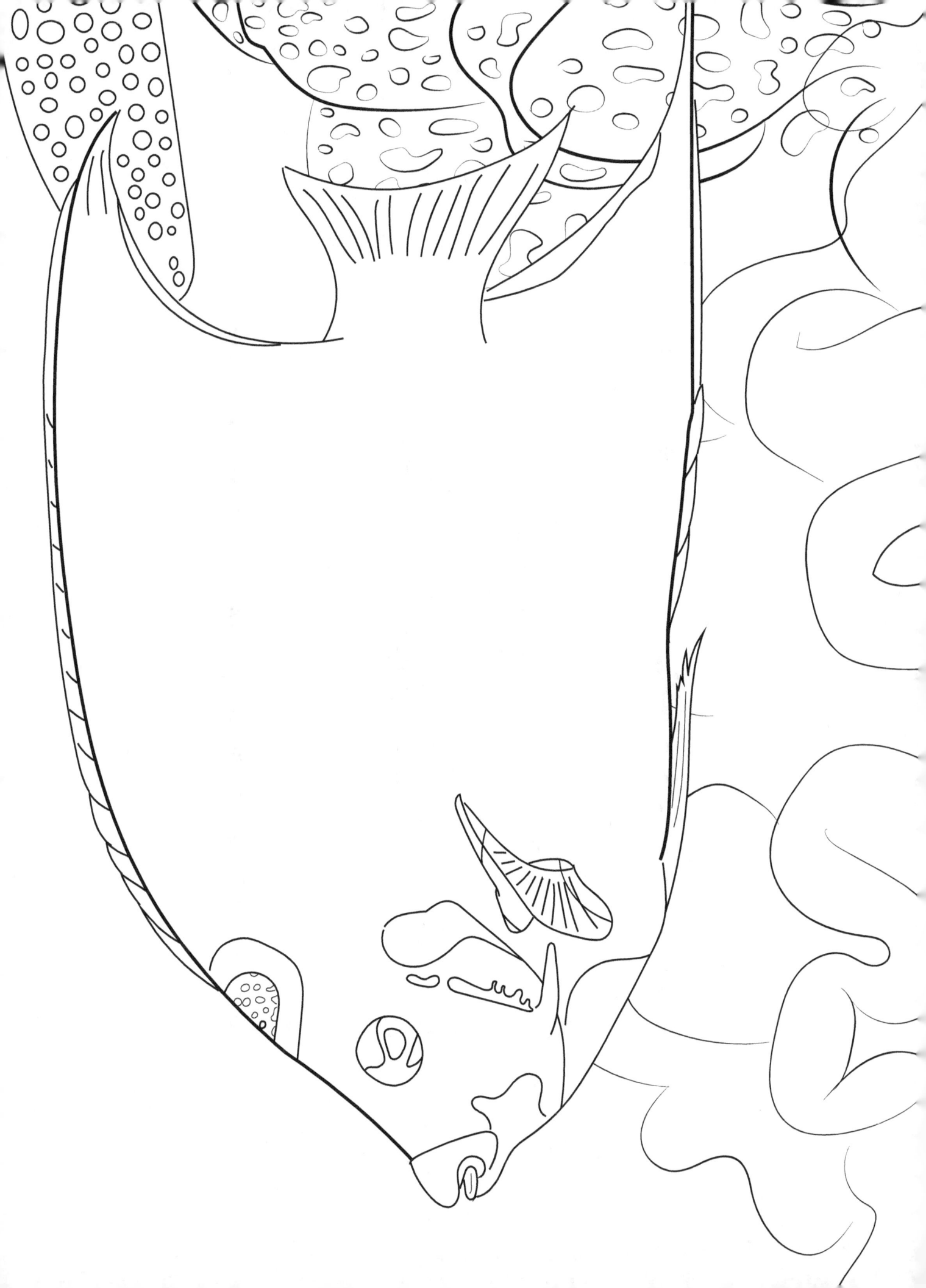

Queen Angelfish

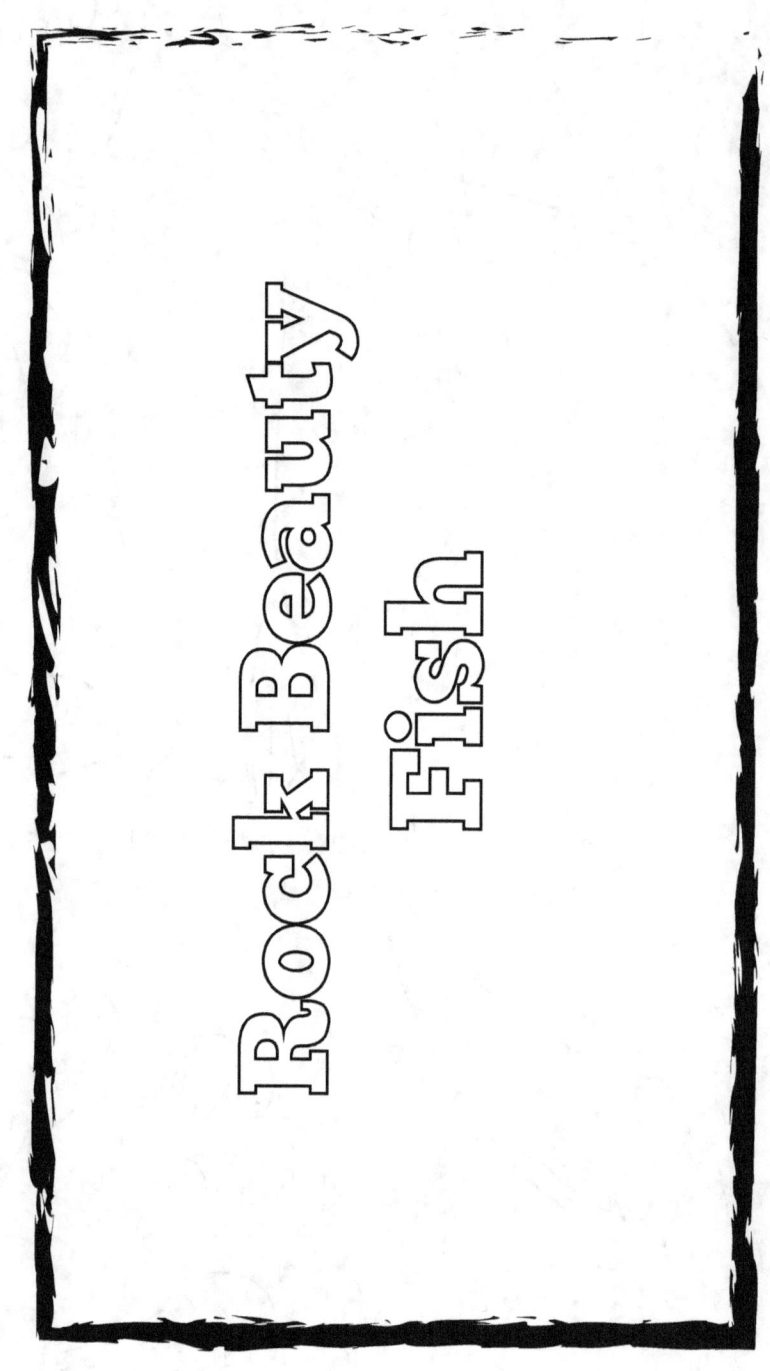

Rock Beauty
Fish

Yellow Tang

Banded Butterflyfish

Bluehead Wrasse

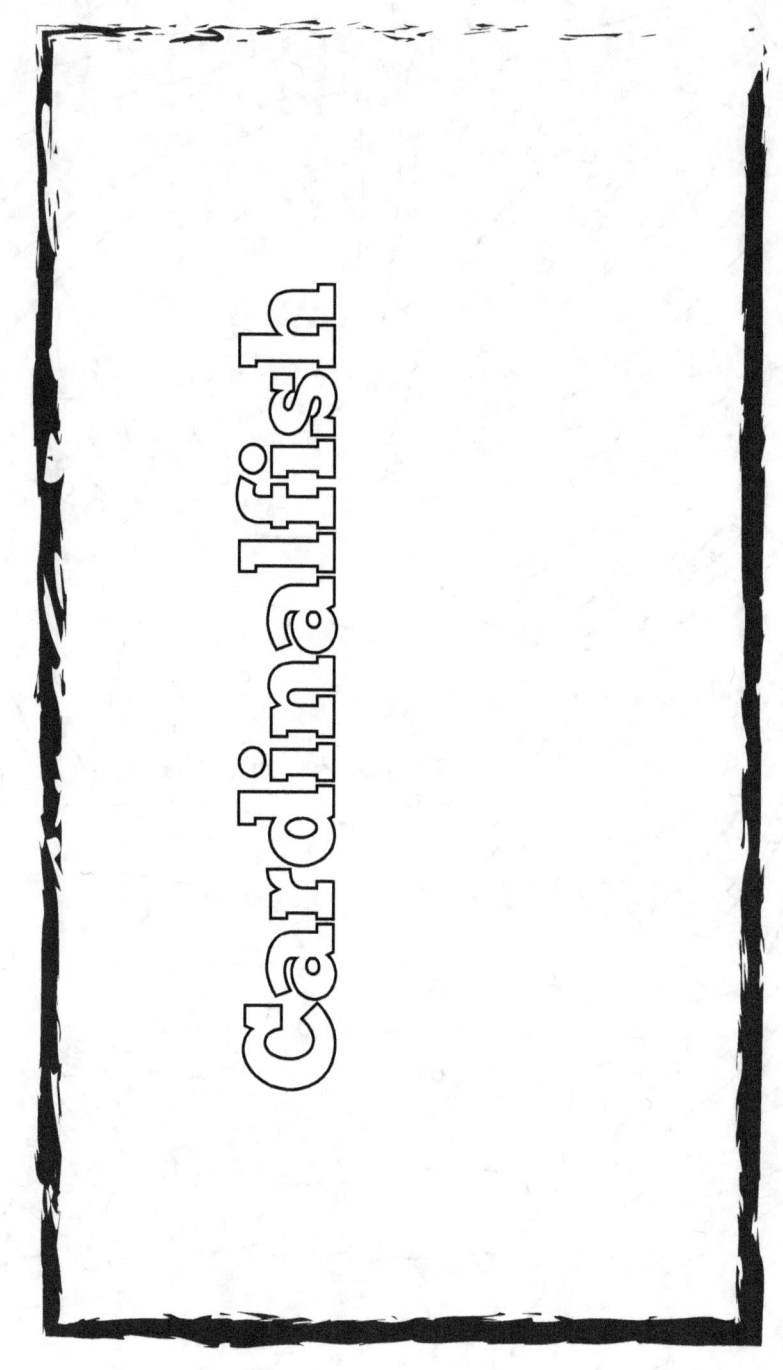

Cardinalfish

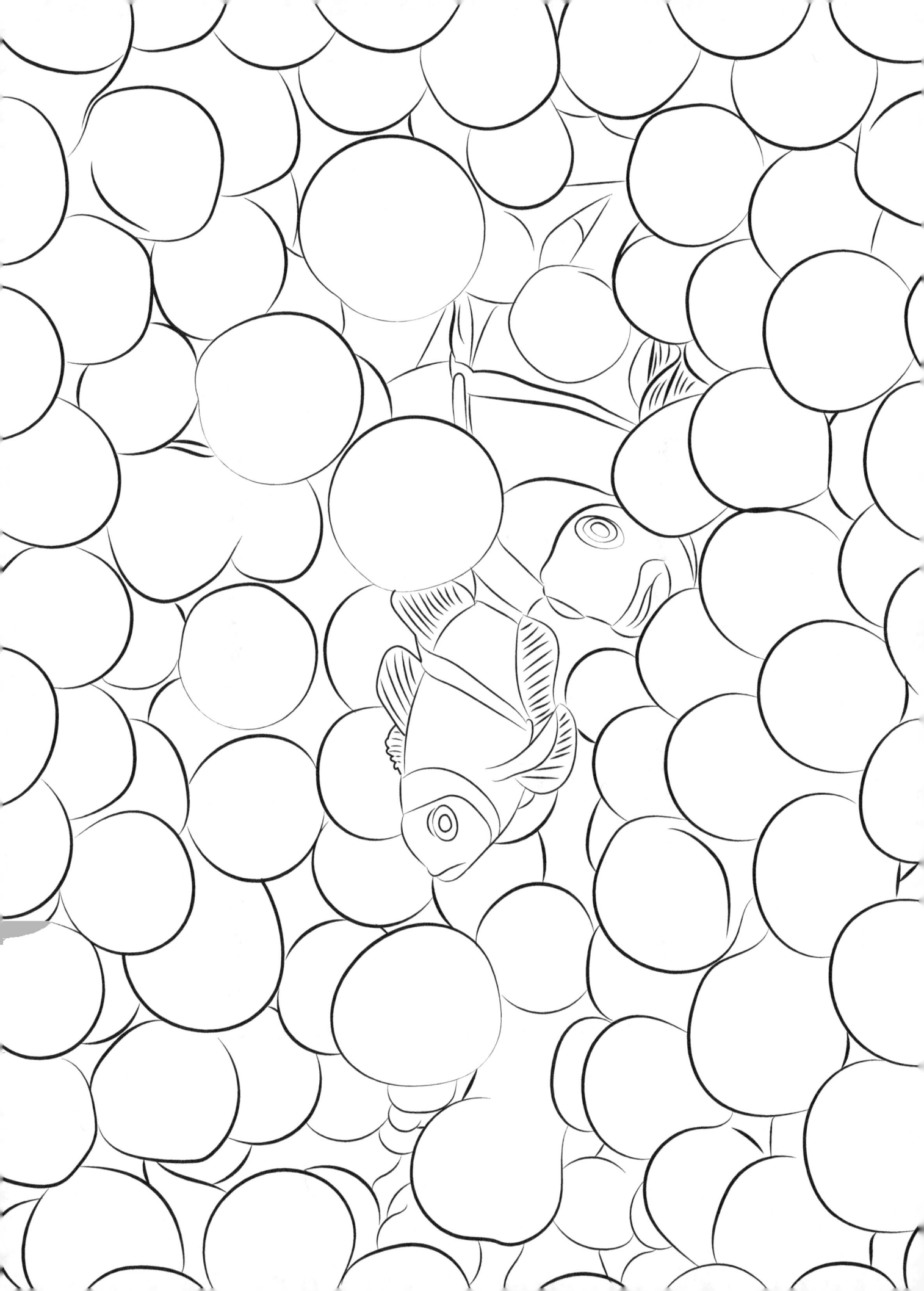

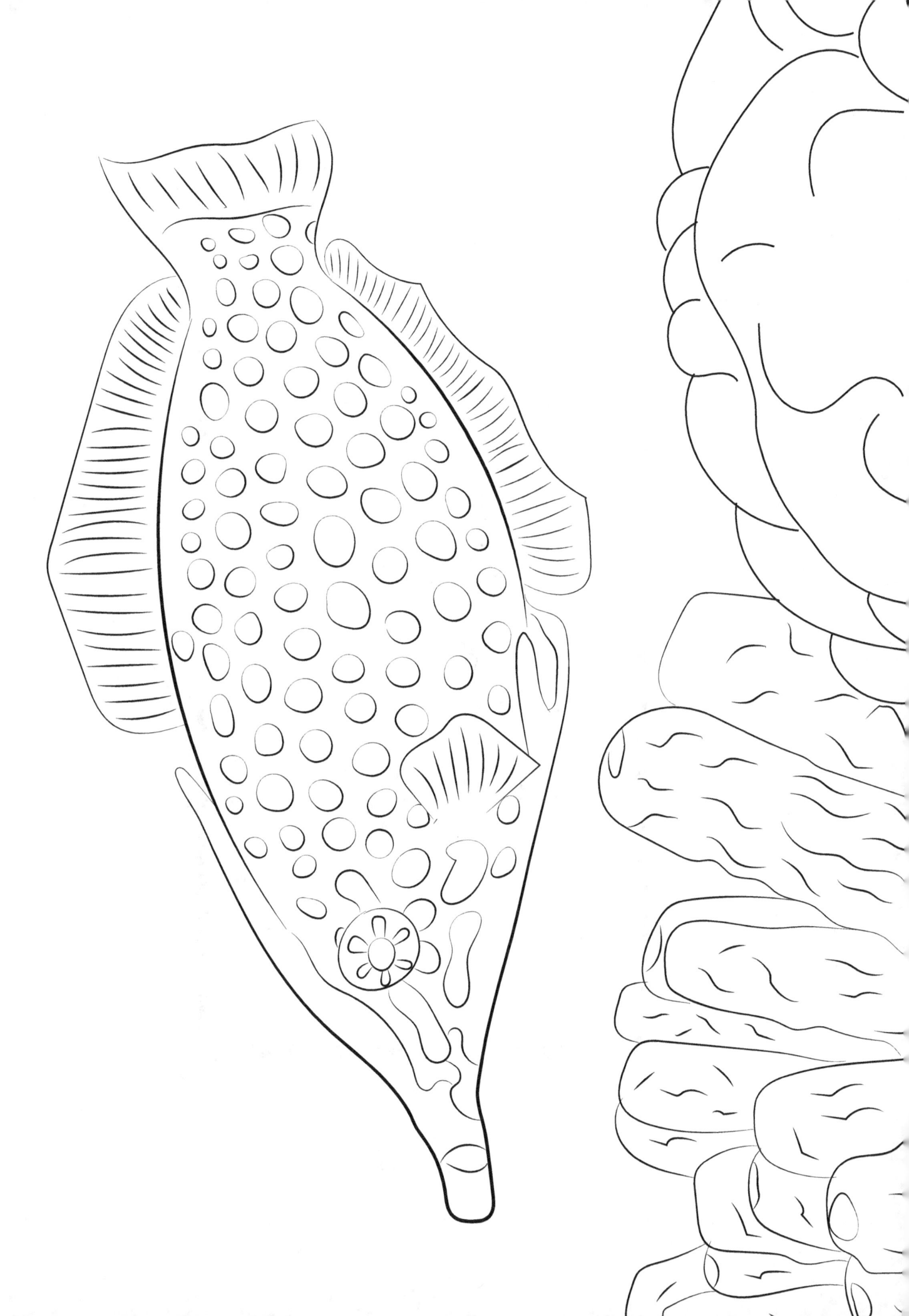

Filefish

Flame Angelfish

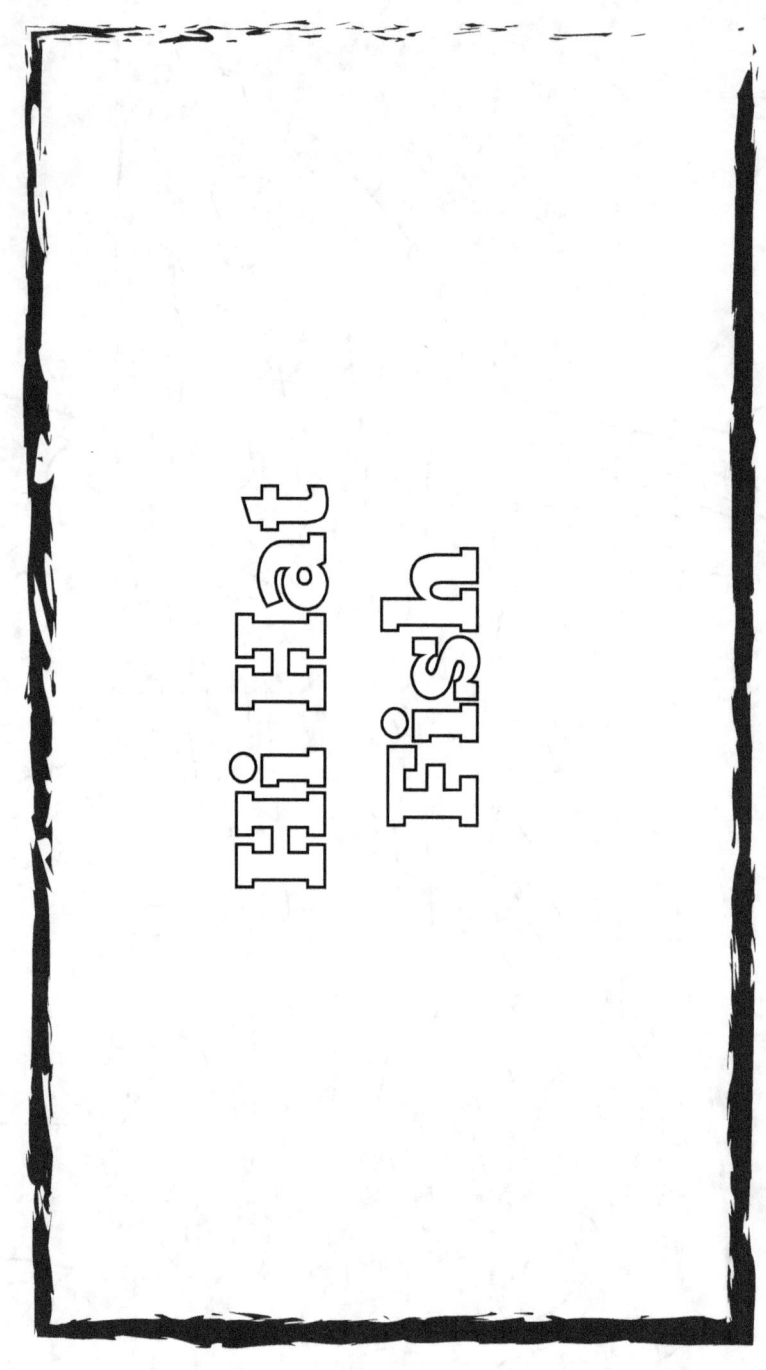

Lionfish

Mandarin Fish

Moorish Idol

Fish

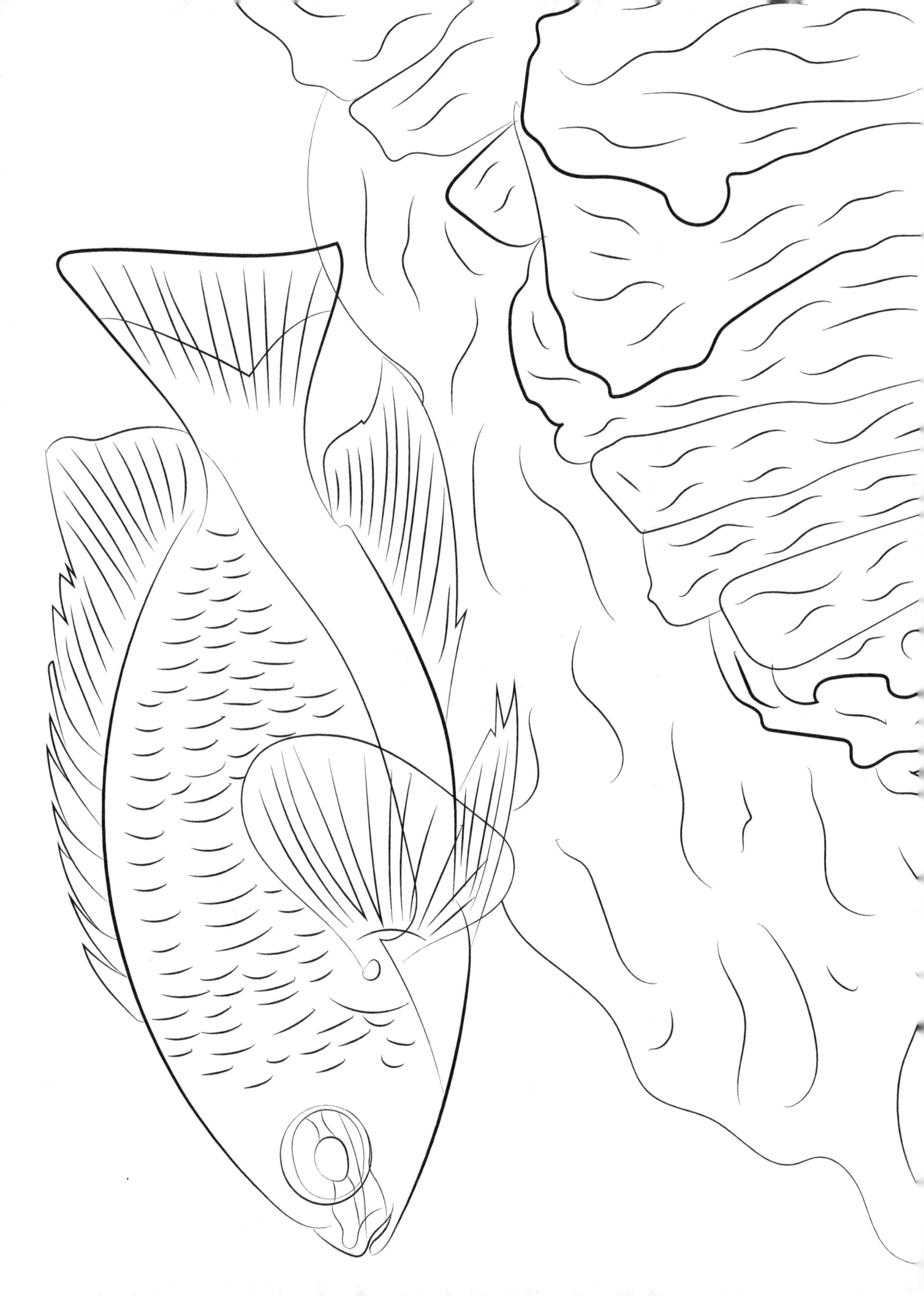

Neon Dmaselfish

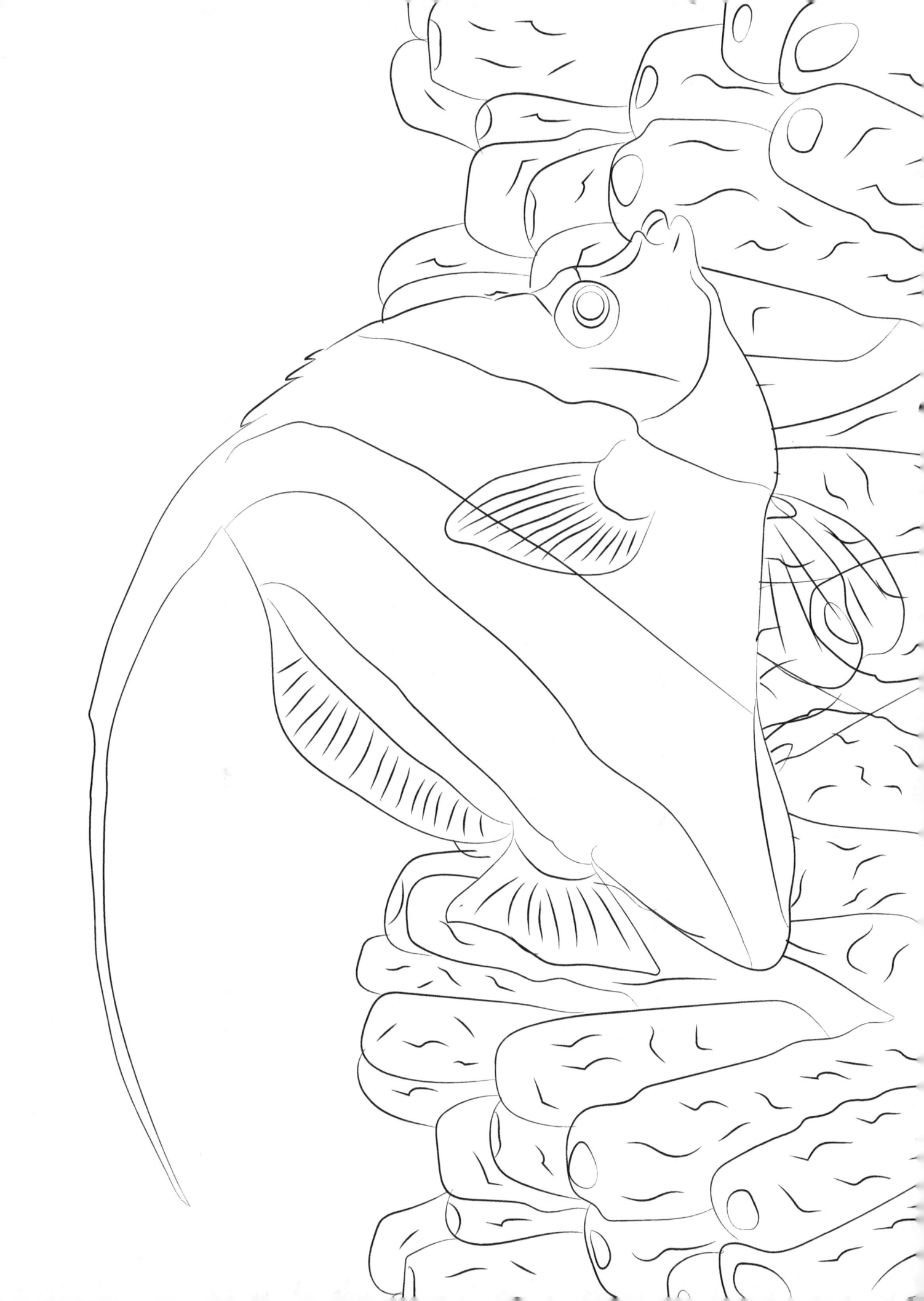

Pennant Coralfish

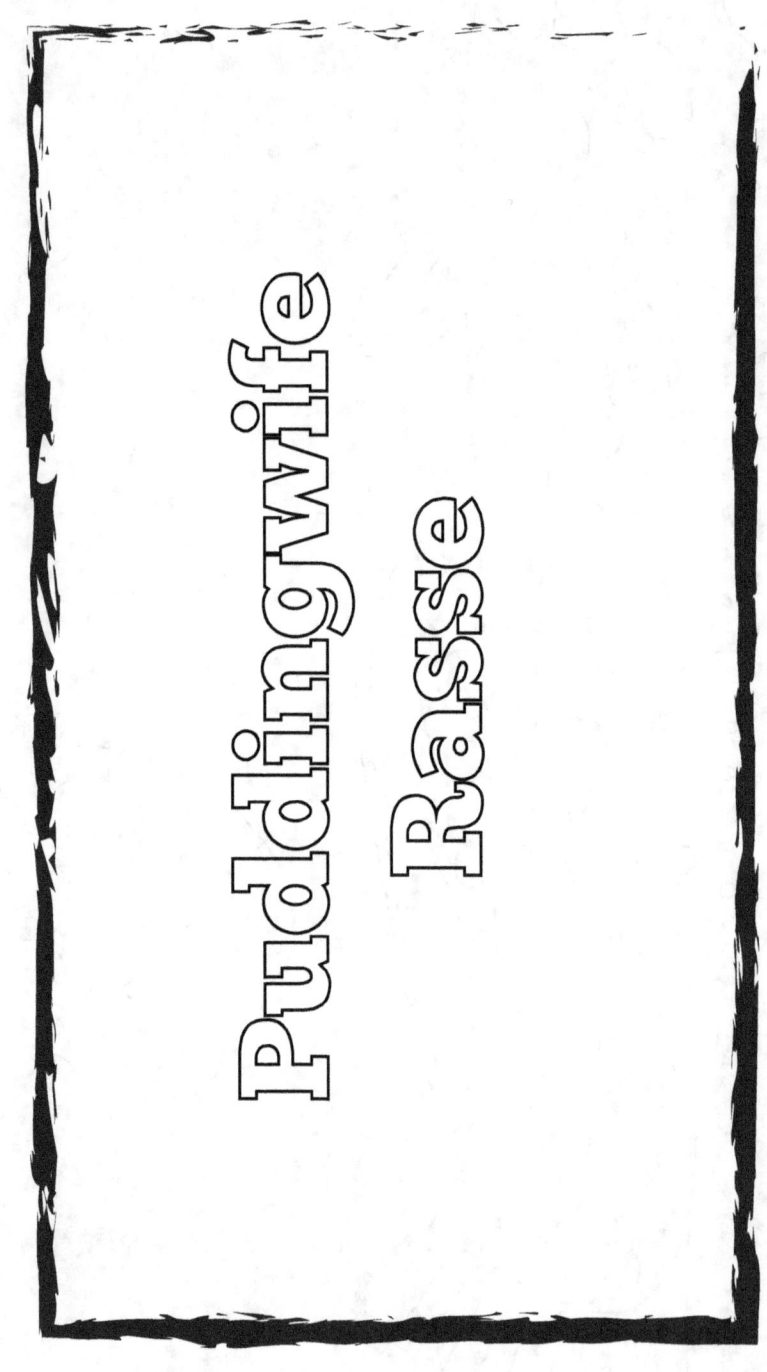

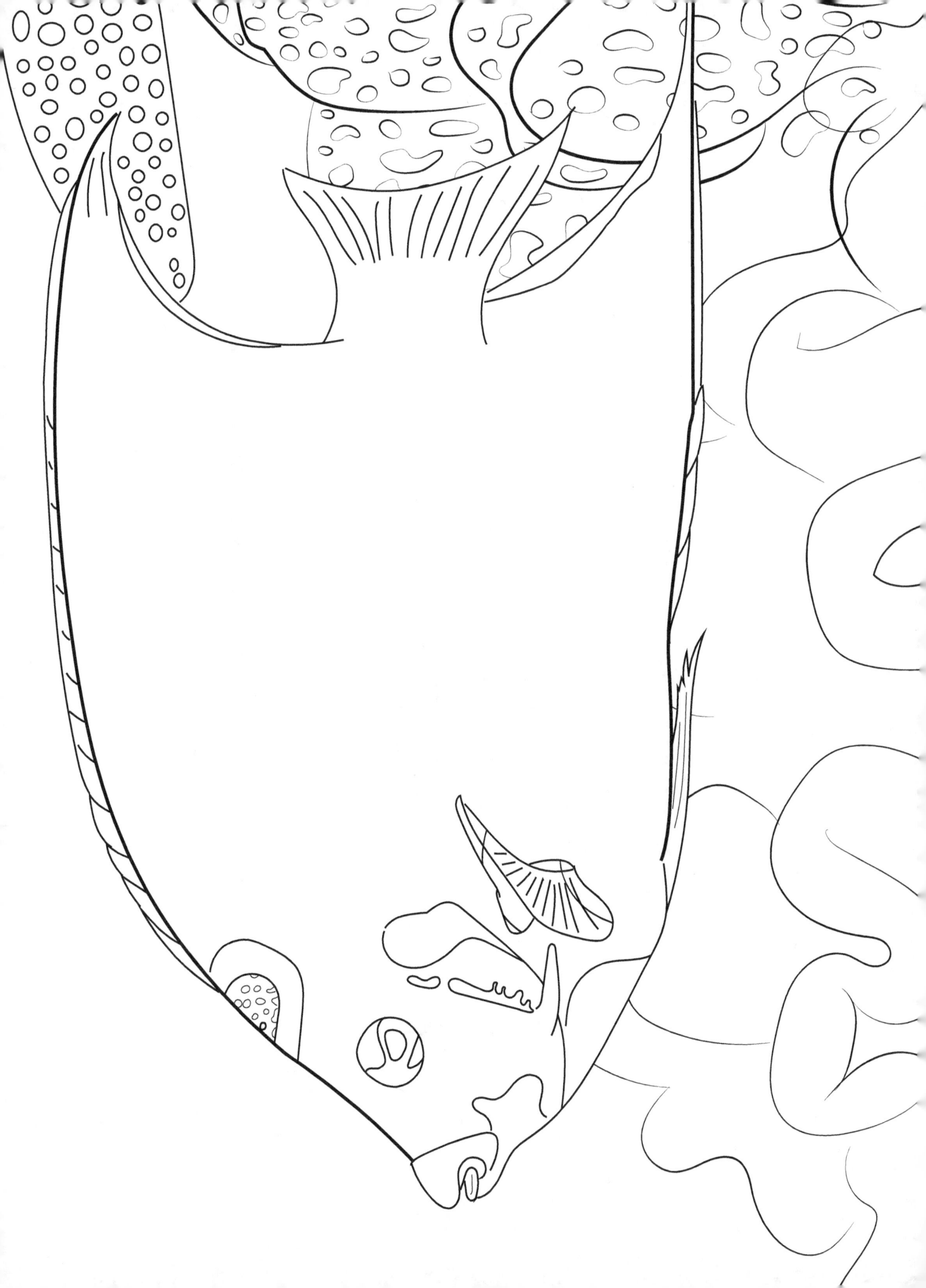

Queen Angelfish

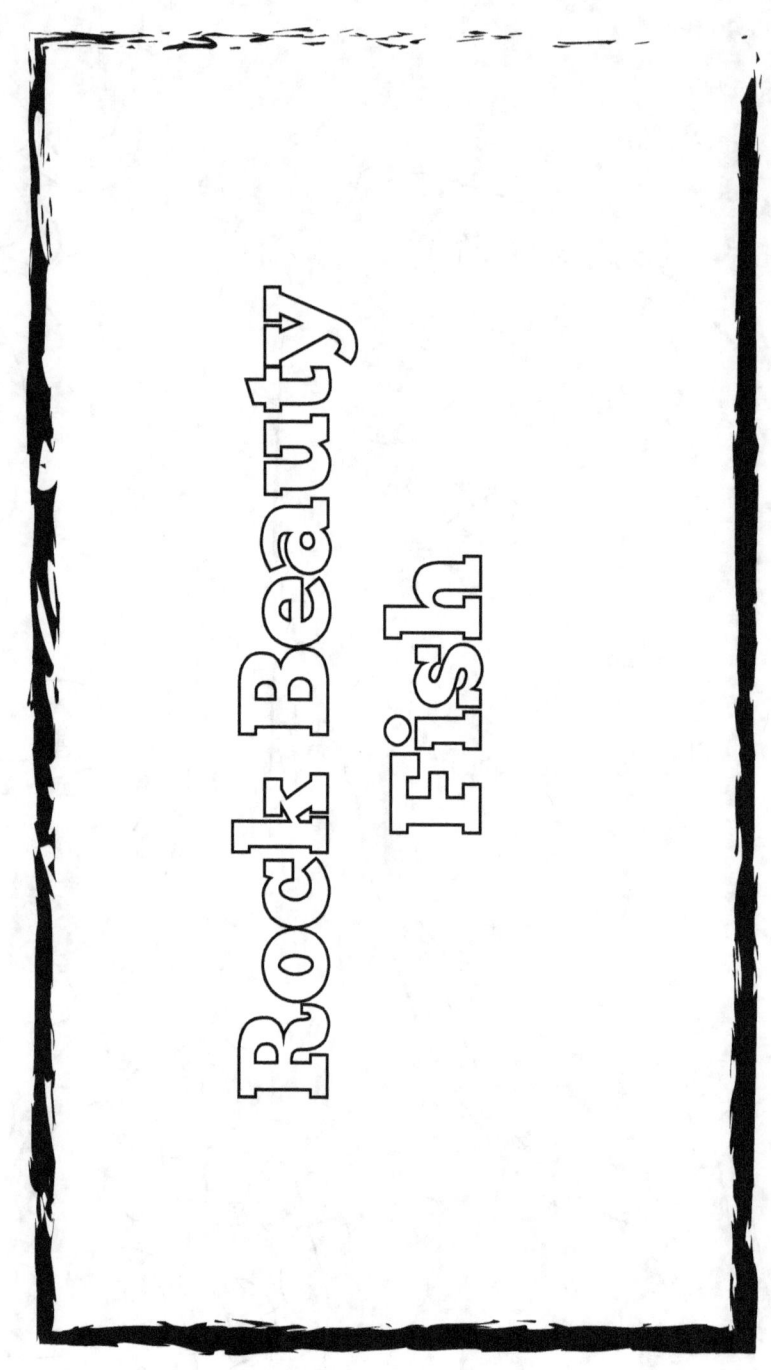

Rock Beauty Fish

www.ingramcontent.com/pod-product-compliance
Lightning Source LLC
Chambersburg PA
CBHW081151280526
45787CB00008B/3292